HOME AND FAMILY DEFENSE

Safeguarding Your Loved Ones and Property
(2023 Guide for Beginners)

Simon Chavez

Home and Family Defense

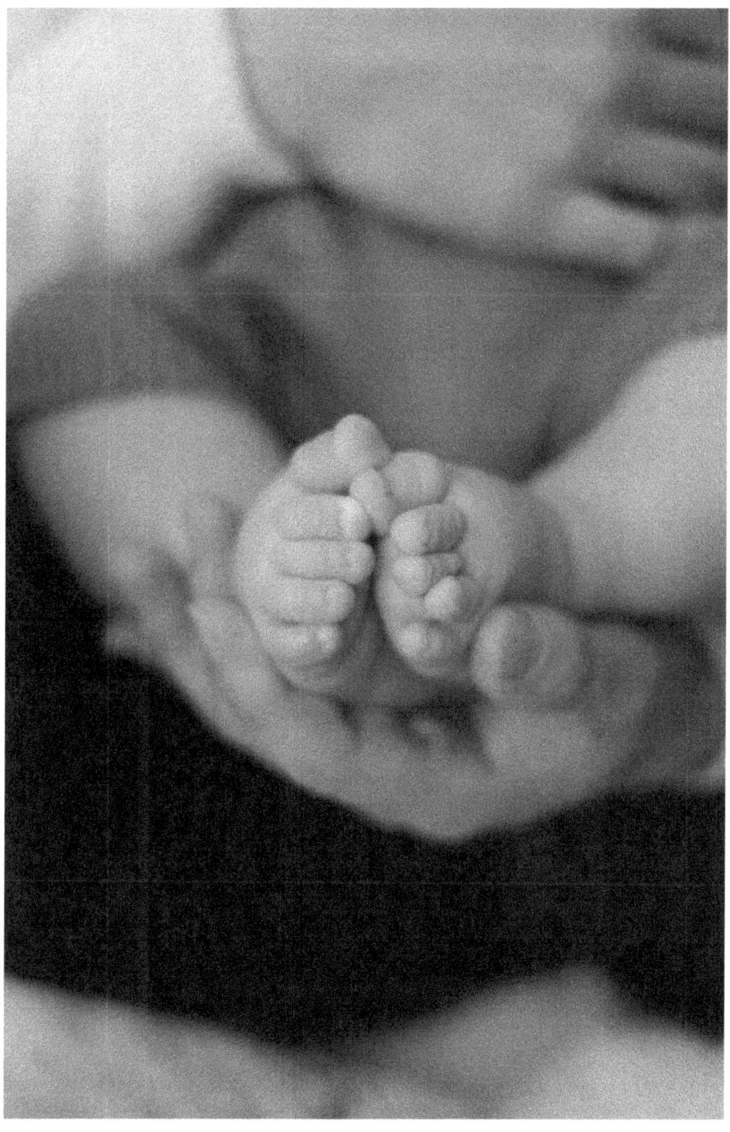

One of your top objectives, both short- and

long-term, should be the protection of your house and your family or group. It makes no difference how much water and food you have stored if you lose everything by not preparing.

being willing to battle for it. Whatever security precautions you put in place before the emergency or disaster happened are likely to be ineffective in a long-term survival scenario; most current security systems are intended to contact authorities and allow authorities to address the problem. Authorities may not even exist in a crisis situation, so we must safeguard our land in other ways.

To create a defense strategy, divide the task into smaller components, such as upgrading your protective structure, collecting defensive weaponry, and installing alarms.

However, while we move through these parts, there is something you should be aware of: OPSEC, or operation security.

Grey Man and OPSEC

OPSEC primarily means not attracting the notice of your neighbors or alerting them to the stuff you have. For example, it is best not to discuss all of the food or supplies you have on hand. The fewer people who know about your riches, the better, and that includes your neighbors. Do not order meals or other preparations every week while you are preparing.

If you do, you should either go to the store personally or purchase it on an as-needed basis from a firm that employs unmarked packaging. This is done so that your neighbors don't see you're preparing and don't come later begging for food, or worse, stealing it. Essentially, keep your preparations under wraps.

Keep your supplies hidden, although that should go without saying. Even if you put them in your basement, away from prying eyes, cover your boxes with drapes or blankets so that your resources are not visible if someone comes in for whatever reason.

Another thing you should consider is your

look. For example, after a few months following a disaster, attempt to seem to have lost weight or to be going through a difficult time like your neighbors. This is because being the only person in the area who has not dropped weight may raise concerns. Obviously, you should not starve yourself. Not only that, but an unshaven face and untidy hair might make you seem less prosperous than your contemporaries. The "Gray Man" technique involves blending in with the crowd. This may seem cruel, but in times of survival, you must occasionally make sacrifices to defend yourself.

Weapons of Defense

Humans have used weapons to protect themselves since the dawn of time. Weapons exist in a variety of shapes and sizes, with some meant to attack and others to protect, but the majority are adaptable, and their function is determined by the wielder. For most of us, the very concept of carrying a handgun, let alone wounding someone with it, is terrifying, but there are many individuals who would shoot without hesitation. This already occurs; imagine what would happen if a disaster struck and society's common sense no longer prevailed.

You may believe that a baseball bat or other short-range weapon would be sufficient for protection, but they are unlikely to defend you against a pistol. If you want to be genuinely prepared, you should have a long-range weapon. You don't need to go out and acquire a sniper, but a pistol or anything more discrete that you can carry with you when you walk outdoors to perform chores is definitely a better option.

Of course, the optimal form of defensive weapon depends on the individual.

Every gun owner has distinct preferences; we will go through the many sorts of weapons so you can make an educated selection. But, before we get there, it's vital to discuss the choice of whether, if ever, to shoot. This is a very difficult choice to make; in fact, there are no recommendations on this subject, and it is entirely dependent on the circumstances. However, some pointers may be useful if the circumstance occurs.

First, choose your goal. Avoid firing the trigger in low-light settings or while under high stress since the mind may play numerous tricks in such scenarios. Always know who or what you're intending to aim at, but also know what's behind the target; you don't want to shoot or strike the incorrect person. Another point to remember while using a gun is that just because there is no rule of law at the moment does not mean you should behave lawlessly. Shoot only when absolutely necessary, and keep in mind that the law may be restored one day, and authorities may pursue crimes committed during such moments of crisis. Finally, if you and your family or group are healthy and safe at the conclusion of a conflict, you have most likely chosen the proper option.

Handguns

Handguns, more than any other kind of handgun, should be selected based on how they fit in your hand and how comfortable you are with them.

This is because the better one sits, the more you will train with it and become more proficient at handling it. So, before buying a pistol, you should test out a couple to see how they fit in your hand.

Handguns are classified into two types: revolvers and semiautomatics. The benefits and drawbacks are entirely dependent on the individual. A revolver is normally simpler to operate than a semi-automatic, but the latter contains more ammunition, so you won't have to reload as often. Calibers that are often utilized include 45, 40, 9mm, and 357. The less common the caliber of a gun, the more difficult it is to locate ammo.

Handguns are the most convenient weapons to carry and operate, making it easier to carry a large amount of ammo.

Handguns are typically medium-range weapons with a shorter reach than other kinds of firearms. Furthermore, the farther away the objective, the more likely you will miss it. A pistol, on the other hand, will be enough to defend your house from an invader.

Rifles

Rifles are intended for long-range shooting. If you want to utilize your weapon for large game hunting, this may be the ideal choice for you, and you can add a sight to make it a sniper rifle. You may camp on the roof of your house and monitor and protect the countryside around you with a sniper rifle. For many people, possessing a.22 rifle is the finest option for survival, owing to its adaptability. It features inexpensive ammo, is simple to use, and is ideal for hunting. Many people argue that a.22 is too low-powered; however, the greater the caliber, the more costly the ammo becomes, so if you're on a budget, a.22 will suffice.

Carbines

Some people mistake carbines for rifles, and they are not mistaken.

They are, nonetheless, quite different from more ordinary guns.

Carbines are essentially rifles with a shorter barrel. Carbines have a bad reputation since they have been used to commit many crimes, yet one of their positives is how scary they are. Aside from that, its large ammo capacity is a significant benefit. However, they are rather costly when compared to other rifles, and their ammo is just as expensive.

The AR-15, SKS carbine, and any form of the AK are the two most popular carbines, mostly because they are dependable and endure a long time, which would be useful in a survival scenario.

Shotguns

Many people feel that shotguns are ideal for home defense. They have excellent close-range powers, and if you use a shotgun round instead of a slug, you won't have to worry about accuracy. This is because shotshells spread as you fire; therefore, if you aim towards the target, you will most likely hit it. However, keep in mind that if you use birdshot ammunition (shotgun ammunition meant to shoot birds), your chances of over-penetrating are reduced. Over-penetrating occurs when a shotgun round is fired and penetrates past the target, placing additional individuals in danger of being shot. This is particularly crucial if you're using it inside your house, since you don't want to strike someone in the next room. These firearms are reasonably priced, and their ammo is similarly reasonably priced and widely available at gun shops. Although they are not the lightest weapons, they are simple to use.

When should you call it quits?

People often concentrate excessively on expanding their arsenal of weapons while ignoring alternative defense methods. So, before you start collecting defensive weapons, establish a strategy and outline your objectives.

Ideally, all adults in your group who are mature enough (this is critical) should have a handgun. When it comes to ammunition, it is difficult to say how much you will need, but it is likely to be between 1000 and 1,500 rounds for firearms, 2,000 to 3,000 shells for shotguns, and between 4,000 and 6,000 if you intend to buy a rifle for both hunting and personal protection. You could hunt with a shotgun or a pistol, but it would be much more difficult.

Other Armaments

Non-firearm weaponry will be rendered ineffective against guns.

They may, however, be useful as tools. When it comes to knives, you should seek out a full-tang blade with a blade length of 5 to 6 inches. This implies that the knife's blade extends all the way into the handle, increasing its stability. The thickness of the blade is also significant; the thicker the blade, the less likely it is to shatter.

When it comes to the handle, look for something that is comfortable to hold even when wet. You will also need a sheath for the knife, particularly if you want to carry it with you. A basic leather sheath may do for this; just make sure it is comfortable to wear when going about and performing chores. When it comes to knives, it all boils down to how comfortable they are in your hand, but two of the most popular among survivalists are the CSP by Mission Knives and the BOB by TOPS Knives. You should do your own research and analyze all of your possibilities.

Protecting Your Residence

You should concentrate not just on expanding your arsenal of weapons but also on fortifying your residence. There are several ways to defend your home without turning it into a bunker.

The first step is to identify any potential weak areas in your home. Doors and windows are frequently the weakest points in a house, so you should look at ways to strengthen them. When it comes to doors, there are two things you can do right away. Longer screws should be used on the hinges of your outside doors. Normal screws just serve to hold the door in place; by using longer screws, you enable the screw to penetrate the door frame and make it more resistant to forced entry. Adding deadbolts to your doors can help strengthen them.

Boarding your doors and windows may help boost their strength, but this is usually only a viable option for non-used doors and windows. Purchasing a pair of 2x6 boards and screwing them against any disused external door frames might boost security; you can also apply this to your main door frames while barricading yourself inside the home.

Windows may be a major issue, owing to the

fact that they are composed of fragile glass. Even though it will obscure the sun, boarding them is the best option. You may use long screws to connect a measured plywood board to the window frame. Install the plywood on the inside of the window rather than the outside because if a window breaks, the glass will fall outside your home.

Purchase a couple bags of sand from your local landscaping store and arrange them around the home, for example, in front of your higher windows to provide a temporary shooting position. Sandbags may be particularly bullet-resistant.

Defending Your Perimeter

Typically, the perimeter refers to everything outside of your home that is still yours, such as your garden. In a long-term survival scenario, you may wish to expand that perimeter to protect your property. Of

For instance, if you just use pistols and have a large front yard, your perimeter may be significantly reduced.

The fundamental goal of defending a perimeter is to keep danger away from your house or to anticipate circumstances that might become deadly. Perimeter defense is made up of two components: warning systems and systems that dissuade attackers from advancing.

Warning Devices

The sooner you identify an intruder, the better your odds are of minimizing the danger or responding efficiently. As a result, alarm systems are critical. They might be as basic as strings connected to bells or tin cans filled with stones. When the intruder comes into contact with one of the strings, it will create a noise and notify you.

You may go for something less basic and purchase some battery-powered alarms, such as motion sensors; however, make sure you have enough batteries to utilize them for extended periods of time in a survival scenario, at least a few months' worth. If you employ battery-powered motion sensors, do your homework to determine the ideal places for them around your perimeter.

Traps

Because of the time and effort required, particularly if you have a big garden, transforming your garden into a gigantic trap is not a practical solution.

Furthermore, any visit to your yard might be fatal.

Instead, deploy traps deliberately to direct attackers to an area that you can readily protect, a technique known as funneling. This generally entails compelling the invaders to show themselves and not allowing them to remain concealed. If an intruder wants to go from the garden gates to your front door, they will choose the most direct route possible: a straight line. In that instance, you'd want to have debris or anything else that would cause them to detour from that course and into the path of the traps you've set up.

Situational Understanding

This is a growing problem in today's culture. Too many individuals are burying their heads in their phones and becoming entirely unconscious of their surroundings. This is the polar opposite of what you want in a survival scenario. In fact, you want to know when and where someone may be approaching your property. You want to be hyper-aware of everything around you.

If somebody approaches your perimeter, they should be challenged, but you don't want to start shooting right away. Before taking any further action, use diplomacy and ask questions. Another thing to keep in mind, particularly if someone approaches your house, is that they might be a distraction. In other words, they may be diverting your attention away from someone else approaching your perimeter from another direction. You should ideally have enough individuals in your group to cycle through monitoring so that you are constantly aware of what is going on inside your perimeter.

If your organization does not have enough members to take turns and rotate, you might consider obtaining a dog. A well-trained dog can accomplish the work of many humans when it comes to detecting intruders, in addition to being a fantastic friend.

Tools

Although tools may be used for anything, we chose to include them in the home security chapter since they can be highly beneficial for repairing or upgrading sections of your defense. However, we will also discuss additional items that may be useful in a survival emergency.

Before we go into all of the various instruments, it is critical, particularly in a disaster scenario when you cannot buy additional equipment, that you have purchased or acquired high-quality ones. This is critical since the use of these technologies might save your life. Look for branded tools and avoid anything from a cheap shop. Although tools are not as vital as food or water, we should consider and collect them throughout time. Obviously, we will not describe every single tool in existence in this chapter; it would be redundant and would need a long and extensive list; nevertheless, we will discuss the common ones that may be useful in a survival scenario.

One last point to mention about tools is their upkeep. It is critical that you have the ability to repair or maintain your tools, mostly because you cannot just walk to the store and get a new one. Make sure you have spare handles for axes and hammers, as well as whetstones and files for sharpening blades. Also, maintaining some of the instruments we'll be discussing may be more difficult than sharpening a knife; an ax, for example, needs a bit more skill. Before calamity occurs, you should have learned how to properly maintain your various equipment.

Basic Repairs and Tools

If you need repairs done around the house, you won't be able to hire a handyman. You must do the task yourself. Tools may vary depending on what you want to repair, but fundamental tools can typically be applied to most circumstances.

Hammers, for example, are one of those instruments that are always handy and available in a variety of sizes. Make certain that the hammer is of great quality and that the connection between the handle and the head seems firm.

Check that it fits well in your hand. It is a good

idea to get at least two hammers so that you have an additional one in case one breaks or goes missing and so that you can work on a project with two people.

Adjustable wrenches are also essential; having at least a few of them on hand will be beneficial.

When it comes to screwdrivers, you should have a variety on hand. Many duties will be impossible to do without them.

Pliers are another essential tool. They come in a variety of sizes, but a ten-inch plus two or three smaller ones would suffice. The following is a rough list of the tools you will require:

Hammers, screwdrivers, wrench sets, pliers

(at least two or three), duct tape, handsaws, a tape measure, and a flashlight

If you still have power and electricity, a cordless drill will come in handy.

Demolition Equipment

When you think of tools, you think of something you can construct. However, they are occasionally required to disassemble items. Getting rid of garbage or fallen trees will require the use of a range of instruments, including a framing hammer. A framing hammer differs from a standard hammer in that the handle is generally longer and the straight claw at the rear of the head is simpler to manipulate. It's also a good idea to have a few pry bars of various sizes on hand, particularly if you need to open or demolish anything in a small space. When you need to move big objects, a ratcheting device with a handle may be incredibly beneficial. These are often known as come-along wrenches, and you may already have one in your basic tool box.

Cleaning Materials

Cleaning supplies may not be the first thing that comes to mind when building a list of all the stuff you'll need in an emergency, but they're really rather crucial.

Dirt may easily develop in your shelter and degrade your quality of life. Cloths or rags and an all-purpose cleanser should be the first things in your cleaning pack. You are not looking for gleaming floors and glittering windows, yet hygiene is essential and difficult to maintain in an emergency.

If you have carpets in your home, they may be difficult to clean unless you have a carpet sweeper, which cannot be electric. If you have rugs, just take them outside and beat them. Aside from that, all you need to keep things neat is a dustpan and a broom. Here's a handy list of cleaning supplies to have on hand: clothes or rags all-purpose cleaning bleach, vinegar, dustpan, broom, carpet sweeper (if available)

Lighting Equipment

Candles and oil lamps may brighten your house and help you direct yourself at night or while coping with a problem.

However, in addition to being hazardous, they are inefficient when compared to alternative lighting systems. The best option is to invest in a solar-powered light. They are somewhat more costly, but they provide a safer, more dependable source of light.

Glow-in-the-dark lights may also be useful; however, they are not as powerful as solar-powered lights, but they will suffice if your purpose is to indicate a route or produce more ambient lighting.

You can acquire flashlights if you have a means to charge batteries.

Nowadays, you may get ones that use LED light technology, which consumes less energy and provides longer light hours.

Firewood Equipment

You may need to construct a fire in a fireplace or outdoors in a fire pit, which may require the use of particular items. First, you'll need a lot of wood, as well as hand saws and other cutting equipment to help you cut the wood down to size. A bow saw may be quite useful for cutting heavier branches. You'll need at least one excellent axe for the very thick wood. Gardening shears and loppers may be useful for cutting smaller branches, although they are not required. The more firewood equipment you have, the better, since how you chop wood depends on the kind of wood and thickness of the logs and branches you discover. However, if you have these crucial tools, you can complete the task.

Safety Equipment

When using and transporting tools, particularly sharp equipment, the risk of injury is extremely considerable. When you consider that the tools may not be as well kept as they should be, as well as a probable lack of light or anything else associated with a disaster, the possibilities of being wounded increase.

Accidents happen even when all of these parameters are met, so we should include protection gear in our survival packs. Safety goggles or glasses, as well as thick gloves, are essential. If anything flies into your eye, it will be difficult to locate an eye doctor. The gloves will protect you from any wounds or splinters that may get infected.

If you are going to be dealing with sawdust, smoke, or even fumes, you should bring some face masks. You should ideally be looking for N95 masks. The following is a list of useful protective equipment.

thick gloves, dust masks, and safety goggles

steel-toe boots and ear protection (if needed).

Communication Instruments

In a disaster-stricken environment, having access to information is incredibly valuable. Being unable to exchange or receive information may isolate you, which, apart from being very stressful, can be detrimental to long-term survival.

Communication gadgets, of course, need electricity, which might be a concern. Because these gadgets are often battery-powered, having a supply on hand is critical. Let's have a look at the numerous communication choices accessible to you.

Two-way Radio

Two-way radios are similar to the walkie-talkies you used to play with as a child, and although they have advanced greatly since then, they still have drawbacks. For example, their range is limited in comparison to other modes of communication, and any physical obstruction between the two places of communication might create connection troubles.

There are two kinds of two-way radios: general mobile radio service (GMRS) and family radio service (FRS). These are the many frequencies that radios may operate on. To use GMRS, you must have a license; however, to transmit over the FRS channels, you do not. Some gadgets enable you to broadcast on both of these frequencies. The range of these gadgets is limited; depending on your surroundings, a mile seems to be their maximum.

The fewer people and items between the two radios, though, the better. For example, they would be more effective in the countryside than in the city. You may buy a static unit for your shelter and a couple portable ones with a lesser range to optimize their range. These are useful when you need to move outside your perimeter for hunting or searching but still want to communicate with the rest of your crew.

Amateur radio operators

Amateur radio, often known as ham radio, may be one of the most useful technologies for long-distance communication. You will need a license, but you should strongly consider acquiring one since ham operators are excellent at sharing information, particularly during times of crisis. There are ham operators in every state and county, and you may contact some of them to help you get started. Furthermore, by becoming acquainted with the local ham operator community, you will be able to readily establish connections with them in a crisis scenario.

Radio on shortwave

These shortwaves may go across the globe and are excellent for understanding what is going on not just in other nations but also in your own country. A shortwave receiver may be very useful in an emergency, particularly a long-term one.

It is critical to understand how to safeguard your house or shelter and, more importantly, your family from the many hazards that may arise as a consequence of a failed civilization.

Even before a disaster strikes, never divulge your hoard of items. When society is still intact, you may trust your neighbors, but in a catastrophic scenario, they may turn on you. Maintaining a low profile is critical for survival. Furthermore, remember to constantly seem to be in distress in order to keep suspicions at bay.

It is critical to plan ahead of time what defensive weapons would be required in such a case and to purchase them. Even if you are not a fan of guns, they may be necessary in a survival scenario. It is crucial to choose the ideal ones for your individual circumstance as well as understand how to utilize them. However, don't depend just on weapons; you'll also need ammunition, extra knives, and any other low-range weapon.

Fortifying the construction of your shelter may keep strangers out and keep them from stealing your food or injuring you and your family. Setting up warning systems and traps may help prevent this from occurring. Having a dog, for example, may improve situational awareness and detect intruders before you or any primitive alarm system. Remember to teach your dog as well, but keep in mind that you will have another mouth to feed.

You'll need a variety of tools to construct fires, mend objects, and improve your shelter's protection. Communication devices such as radios are essential; they may save your life.

www.ingramcontent.com/pod-product-compliance
Lightning Source LLC
LaVergne TN
LVHW021008200726
843506LV00012B/2233